COMMERCIAL TRANSLATIONS

A Business-Like Approach to
Obtaining Accurate Translations

Godfrey Harris
and
Charles Sonabend

The Americas Group
9200 Sunset Blvd., Suite 404
Los Angeles, CA 90069

ISBN 0-935047-01-8 (Hardcover)
ISBN 0-935047-02-6 (Softbound)

Library of Congress Catalog Card Number 85-072415
Includes Index

COMMERCIAL TRANSLATIONS

A Business-Like Approach to
Obtaining Accurate Translations

Table of Contents

A look at Biblical translations · The importance of literary translations · Commercial translations as a cultural necessity · Documents requiring translation · How translators are chosen in comparison to lawyers and accountants · How Americans tend to handle complex subjects in English · What happened to a Pepsi translation.

FOREWORD

COMMERCIAL TRANSLATIONS

FOREWORD

This book on
commercial translations
has been prepared
to help business people
avoid the cost and frustration
of becoming part of any of the
scenes portrayed on
the following
pages.

COMMERCIAL TRANSLATIONS

Scene I

An Architect's Office in New York City.

Partner: Did we get the comments in on our bid from that city in Switzerland?

Associate: Yes, sir, they arrived by courier this morning.

Partner: Are we still in the running for the project?

Associate: We don't know yet. The comments are in German. Steve's out trying to find someone to read them to us.

Partner: How long do we have to respond?

Associate: 'Till the end of this week.

Partner: Why in the devil didn't they send their comments in English?

Associate: I guess because they speak Swiss German there.

Scene II

A Studio in Los Angeles.

Agent: The deal's tight. All we have to do is guarantee that we'll have a dubbing script ready in Danish and Finnish by the start of next quarter.

Producer: Where're we going to get that done?

Agent: I don't know. Maybe I'll find someone at a consulate to moonlight for us.

Producer: Can they do the job?

Agent: They're supposed to know all of those languages.

Producer: Who cares about the Danish and Finnish markets anyway? We never have before.

Agent: Our European distributor.

Scene III

A Computer Manufacturer in Chicago.

President: When are we going to ship the D-450's to Kuwait?

Product Manager: They want us to have the instructions in Arabic first.

President: Is someone working on that?

Product Manager: We took the English material to an Egyptian student at Community College. He says he'll try to get right to it after Finals.

President: Wonderful! Those guys in the Orient will probably have their own machine on the market by then.

Scene IV

A Lawyer's Office in Wichita.

Lawyer: Look, take it downstairs and give it to Virginia. She's got a maid from Turkey.

Secretary: But I think Virginia said she's Armenian.

Lawyer: Well, she probably learned some Turkish in school.

Secretary: Maybe not.

Lawyer: Someone in this town must be able to translate the thing.

Secretary: Let me check the major ads in the yellow pages.

Lawyer: That's fine. I can't just walk into the board meeting tomorrow without even a clue as to whether we have a product liability suit or a new office lease on our hands.

Scene V

A Telephone Conversation in Seattle.

Client: What about by Wednesday?

Translator: I'll try. But it means setting aside the article I'm doing for Professor Steele and that's late as it is.

Client: Wednesday cuts it short enough. We still have to collate your translation with the engineering drawings and get the Chairman's signature on the cover letter.

Translator: What cover letter? I haven't seen that yet.

Client: It's on the way. The political consultants have the draft for final review.

Translator: How many pages are we talking about?

Client: I think they're figuring five to seven.

Translator: Oh, my. That means night work and my wife has theater tickets on Monday.

Client: We're really counting on you to get it all done.

Translator: What if I get sick or one of the kids has a friend over?

Client: Then we may blow four months of work and a
                    shot at a $75 million project.

Translator: I'll do my best. I just hope it's good enough to do
                    it right.

Client: So do we.

Scene VI

A Brokerage House in Boston.

Assistant: All Known Languages Ltd says the invitation is for "lunch and games" at the Finance Minister's summer residence.

Managing Director: Any hint of what that's supposed to involve?

Assistant: The one translator at All Known Languages Ltd says the invitation isn't really clear to him. You're supposed to bring either a sweater and pants in a bag or wear a baggy sweater and pants.

Managing Director: Anything else?

Assistant: Would you want All Known to handle the RSVP?

Managing Director: Not if their translator can't figure out the difference between baggy pants and pants in a bag.

Obtaining accurate, consistent
and timely translations
into a multiplicity of languages
has become an integral part
of international business today.

Unfortunately, most business
people simply don't realize
the importance that a translation
can have on the success or failure
of international transactions.

Many have no idea how to
assess a translator's skills
for a particular
translation need; and very few
have developed the kind of
relationship with a
translator to make him or her
a part of an effective
business team.

This book is specifically designed
to help people understand
and supervise the
translation work
they need done.

SOME GENERAL THOUGHTS ON TRANSLATIONS

The variety of bibles portrayed suggests the extent to which this book has been translated into English as well as other languages.
[Gregrey Harris Photography]

SOME GENERAL THOUGHTS
ON TRANSLATIONS

Perhaps no other published work has been translated as often or as extensively as the Holy Bible. For all the care and scholarship devoted to this book, many questions still arise concerning the accuracy and quality of the *English* translations used by millions of people.

Take, for example, a passage from the Old Testament's Book of Isaiah (7:14), with emphasis we have added:

> "Therefore the Lord himself shall give you a sign; Behold, a *virgin* shall conceive, and bear a son, and call his name Immanuel."
> [King James Version, 1611]

> "Therefore the lord himself will give you a sign. Behold, a *young woman* shall conceive, and bear a son, and shall call his name Imman'u-el (God is with us)."
> [Revised Standard Version, 1952]

Were the words in Isaiah actually a prophecy of the birth of Jesus as later described in the New Testament (Matthew 1:18)? Or did the King James Version merely adopt errors in the Greek translation of the original Hebrew and Aramaic?

The theological implications of these questions are as important as they are fascinating. But here only the variation in the two translations is appropriate to illustrate the significant impact that this particular field of scholarship can have on our thoughts and attitudes.

Peter Glassgold, chairman of PEN American Center's Translation Committee, sees translators as "cultural mediators". Their responsibility, he thinks, is to bridge the inevitable gaps in understanding whenever language barriers must be crossed.

B. J. Chute, one of the founders of the Translation Committee, asks college students to guess how many literary classics would remain on their bookshelves if all translated works were to disappear.

It was not, however, until the Middle Ages that translation of books into English could be supported by a middle class rich enough to afford manuscripts and confident enough to do without a knowledge of Latin grammar. Geoffrey Chaucer, the first great English poet, also became the first great English language translator.

Commercial translations to and from English are proving no less important than literary translations in their effect on our lives. In a modern business environment, the ability to communicate in writing consistently, accurately, and quickly across linguistic barriers has become a commercial imperative.

It is also a cultural necessity. Sophisticated foreigners know that they should not present white flowers to a Japanese hostess – they signify sympathy rather than appreciation – or give clocks in China – they imply that time has run out on a relationship.

Business people must be just as sensitive to the culture of language:

- A selling phrase in France may not work nearly as well in Quebec;

- A Flemish translation is not always useable in Holland.

- Arabic expressions in different Middle Eastern countries are often dependent on the identity of their former occupying power – the British in Egypt, the Italians in Libya, the French in Lebanon.

Too often, though, the fundamental need for commercial translations is either being ignored or slighted – relegated by many to an afterthought or delegated by them to a clerical function. Yet the accurate meaning of translated words for:-

- advertisements
- articles
- brochures
- cables
- catalogues
- contracts
- decals
- instructions
- invoices
- keyboards
- letters
- manuals
- memoranda
- prompts
- records
- scripts
- signs
- stencils
- subtitles

– can be as crucial to the overall success of any business undertaking as the subject matter itself.

> • Why is it that company executives know instinctively that their own lawyers ought to review a contract drafted by outsiders before they authorize its approval?

> • Why is it that public companies are required to obtain independent audits of the books and records maintained by their own accounting staffs?

The answer to these questions, of course, is to ensure that the documents actually and accurately convey what they purport to convey before a dispute arises, a financial commitment is made, or an irrevocable action is taken.

When it comes to the written translation of business documents, however, these same executives may give the task to an employee, a relative, or even a neighbor. Unfortunately, none of these people is likely to have any special competence to do a particular translation task other than a facility for, or familiarity with, the foreign language involved.

Translations by amateurs have always been a source of delight to native speakers. *The Saturday Evening Post* recently published a collection of English language signs seen in shops and hotels in Europe:

> • "Dresses for Street Walking"

> • "Come Inside and Have a Fit"

- "Because of the impropriety of entertaining guests of the opposite sex in the bedroom, it is suggested that the lobby be used for this purpose."

- "[Hospital] Visitors: Two to a bed and a half an hour only"

Even when professional translation assistance is sought by a business, the search for a qualified service generally starts and stops with a trip through a local yellow page directory. Unfortunately, the largest ad displayed does not necessarily signify the most competent firm for a particular translation task.

While legal and accounting appointments can consume exhaustive hours of research and reference checks, translators are just as often selected on the basis of their per word fee, their estimate of turn-around time, and their physical location. Movie producers, for example, can spend millions of dollars on a film project over a three-year to five-year period, only to quibble about a few hundred dollars and an extra day or two to translate the finished script for subtitles.

Questions dealing with the background, education, or experience of a translator are all but ignored when selections are made in this area of specialty. Yet these same questions are usually asked of every other professional from architects to zoologists.

This pattern is even more surprising when compared to how many American executives react to a technical paper in a field unfamiliar to them. They generally ask some independent specialist to evaluate its meaning – even if the paper itself is written in English.

COMMERCIAL TRANSLATION

The following excerpt is taken from a 1984 report provided to a Southern California real estate development company by an environmental consulting firm:

> "Experimental work has been conducted on disturbances in the intertidal zone relative to recolonization and algal succession in sewage impacted areas ... this work ... demonstrated that bluegreen algae, filamentous green algae, and colonial diatoms are early successional and opportunistic organisms of upper shoreline areas... These early colonizers will remain as immature, low diversity, subclimax communities."

Upon receipt of the report, the real estate executives submitted it to government experts for review. These experts confirmed that the report found no danger to the area's existing marine life if the project under consideration were to proceed.

Yet, these very same business executives have acknowledged that they probably would not have hesitated to give the same document – had it been written in Spanish – to someone on their staff who merely happened to *speak* that language.

They would have assumed, as do most of us, that if an educated individual can converse fluently in a foreign language, he or she will also be able to understand – for purposes of translation or evaluation – the precise vocabulary and exact import of anything that might be written in that language.

If such an assumption isn't valid in English, why should it be any more true in a foreign language? More importantly, such an assumption can turn out to be costly or embarrassing or both.

Most people forget that translating from one language to another is as precise and as specialized a skill as possessed by those employed in the drafting of the original material itself.

The Pepsi Cola company recently learned this point the hard way:

> On billboards across Taiwan, its famous slogan – "Come alive with the Pepsi generation" – was rendered into Chinese as: "Pepsi will bring your ancestors back from the dead."

This book is designed to help executives understand the complexities involved in foreign language translations and to assist them in the selection of an appropriate commercial translation service for the tasks they have at hand.

THE
EXPLOSION
OF
LANGUAGES
USED
IN
INTERNATIONAL
COMMERCE

A sampling of the flags in front of the UN secretariat building in New York illustrates the variety of languages in use in international affairs today.
[United Nations Photo]

THE EXPLOSION OF LANGUAGES USED
IN INTERNATIONAL COMMERCE

One glance at a statistical profile of the world's languages and their current usage patterns suggests why accurate and consistent translations must become an integral part of every business transaction across linguistic barriers:

- Approximately *3000* different languages are in daily use in the world today.

- The Special Libraries Association's *Directory of Translators and Translation Services* catalogues capabilities to and from English in *75* different languages. Among the ones that could be required in business today are:

> Afghan
> Afrikaans
> Arabic
> Armenian
> Azerbaijani
>
> Basque
> Bengali
> Burmese
>
> Cambodian
> Catalan
> Celtic
> Chinese
> Czech
>
> Danish
> Dutch
>
> Eskimo
> Estonian
> Ethiopian

COMMERCIAL TRANSLATIONS

Finnish
Flemish
French

Gaelic
Georgian
German
Greek

Hebrew
Hungarian

Icelandic
Italian

Japanese
Javanese

Korean

Laotian
Latvian
Lithuanian

Macedonian
Malay
Moldavian
Mongolian

Norwegian

Persian
Polish
Portuguese
Provencal

Romanian
Russian

Serbo-Croat
Siamese (Thai)
Slovak
Slovenian
Spanish
Swahili
Swedish

Tagalog
Tamil
Turkish

Ukrainian
Urdu
Uzbec

Vietnamese

Welsh

Yiddish

- The first 75 Nobel prizes awarded for literature were written by authors working in 18 different languages.

- Scientific and technical publications with worldwide interest are now published in 50 different languages.

- American and British computer companies have found that they regularly write screen messages, keyboard information, and instruction manuals in 9 foreign languages: Danish, Dutch, Finnish, French, German, Italian, Norwegian, Spanish, and Swedish. Some are also routinely preparing Arabic, Hebrew, and Japanese versions as well.

- The first complete dictionary of the English language was compiled in 1750 and included some 43,000 words; in 1973, the Shorter Oxford English Dictionary totaled approximately 163,000 words. The Conseil International de la Langue Française estimates that 3000 words are added to the French language each year.

COMMERCIAL TRANSLATIONS

- The United Nations translates from and into six languages – Arabic, Chinese, English, French, Russian, and Spanish. But if all languages spoken by citizens of all member states were to be translated into every other language, it is estimated that some 9 million translation teams might be required.

- The largest administrative expense of the European Economic Community – accounting for approximately one-third of the organization's costs – is said to be for translation services. It promises to grow even more as the Community expands to 12 members with the addition of Spain and Portugal.

- The U.S. Department of State currently employs 24 full-time translators in Washington, D.C., and uses some 200 more under contract; it is estimated that the Department annually spends in excess of $10 million on its translation requirements.

- At last count, about 300 U.S. universities and colleges now offer translation programs at both the undergraduate and graduate levels.

With language usage growing – and with the languages themselves expanding – translations have become an important element in world commerce. The European Economic Community calculates that the demand for translation work is increasing at a rate of 10% per year and that more that 150 million pages are now being translated annually by some 175,000 professional translators.

THE EXPLOSION OF LANGUAGES USED IN INTERNATIONAL COMMERCE

Until the 1960s, American businesses could treat translations as they treated most other international matters – with an ignorance born of unfamiliarity. In those days, the United States was said to be economically self-sufficient in almost everything except bananas and coffee.

Most American business people didn't really need to know much about what was occurring commercially abroad to stay well ahead of their foreign competitors. That, of course, has all changed in the last 25 years. (Readers may wish to review Scene II in the Foreword. It illustrates the kind of change that has affected many different U.S. businesses.)

Today, almost 18% of the U. S. gross national product – some $600 billion a year – is dependent on goods flowing into or out of the country. The United States now owes more money to foreign individuals and institutions than it is owed by them.

While others had to learn how to speak and write accurately in English after World War II if they wanted to do business in the United States, Americans are only now realizing that they must communicate efficiently in foreign languages if they hope to compete effectively with other international firms at home and abroad.

A Los Angeles-based firm clearly had that point reinforced when it received a letter from a company in Hamburg. After haltingly expressing in English its interest in a particular product offered by the American firm, the letter closed with the following plea:

> "Please send me your know-how detailed and your idea of price per piece. If its (sic) possible, please send me your offer in German (especially for this I would be very thankful.)"

In another example, a Belgian firm recently lost a follow-on contract to supply additional tooling machines to a major West German manufacturer. The Belgian company reportedly had failed to conduct its business dealings with the manufacturer in German. The manufacturer specifically cited language as the reason for not buying the additional machines from the Belgian supplier.

Americans are also becoming well aware of the fact that it is one thing to learn a foreign language at school or practice it on trips to other countries. It becomes an entirely different matter when these same Americans try to use their limited language skills in business dealings with someone whose native tongue is the one they studied.

Moreover, as increasingly complex trading patterns develop, the need for multiple linguistic capabilities becomes more obvious:

- In the French electronics firm that assembles Japanese and Taiwanese components into finished products in Mexico for the American market.

- In the Canadian-owned, Luxembourg-based trading firm that buys Polish products for various countries on the Arabian peninsula.

- Among Norwegian shipbuilders who construct supertankers for Hong Kong firms that register the vessels in Panama to carry crude petroleum between Kuwait and Korea.

In all probability, these kinds of multi-country transactions were originally conceived and communicated in English. But what about the languages used in the documents that support these transactions:

• In the legal documents that come to bind the parties and subcontractors to each other?

• In the instructions that must guide a Spanish-speaking worker in his responsibility to test the compatibility of two components manufactured in different countries in the Orient?

• In the operating manuals that allow Filipino sailors to replace parts for British engines while their ships are docked in a Japanese port?

As a matter of good business practice, all of these types of documents ought to be produced in a multiplicity of languages. Unfortunately, they aren't.

While the world seems to have arrived at a moment in history when the facile use of many languages simultaneously has become an integral part of successful international commerce, few individuals are able to command all of the nuances involved in languages commonly used in business transactions today.

The following story from a book called *The English Game* clearly makes the point about the subtleties of language:

"A Yorkshire truck driver once asked an American diplomat standing outside the U.S. Embassy in London how to get from Grosvenor Square to Picadilly Circus. The American described the streets the truck driver had to find and the turns he had to make.

'Is it a good way?' asked the driver.

'Shouldn't be too much traffic now,' the American said.

'But is it a good way?' the driver insisted.

'It's really the only way *I* know,' the American responded.

'Yes, but is it a good way – say three or four miles?'

'Oh,' sighed the American. 'It's just a few blocks from here.' "

The American, of course, had totally missed the fact that the term "good way" in England refers to the distance involved more often than to the quality of the route.

The importance of linguistic nuances arises most frequently in advertising copy. A Minneapolis-based bank recently hired a market research firm, specializing in content analysis, to review the bank's advertising material.

The research firm's in-depth interviews revealed that customers felt a negative connotation when informed that the bank would "*pay* interest" on checking accounts – ' paying, they found, implies something to be avoided by the average person.

The bank now stresses that these accounts "*earn* interest". Just this simple change to a more positive verb – to describe the same function – is reported to have increased the bank's appeal to new customers.

THE EXPLOSION OF LANGUAGES USED IN
INTERNATIONAL COMMERCE

If errors of understanding or perception can occur when individuals are speaking or reading the *same* language, imagine how many more are possible when they are dealing with *different* languages?

Most American firms are not yet prepared to deal confidently with the language aspects of international commerce. For many business people new to foreign trade transactions, it may seem enough that they have mastered such matters as irrevocable letters of credit, FOB freight quotations, metric measurements, telex codes, customs regulations, and the daily differences in value between a French franc and a Swiss franc.

Now these same business people are asked to grapple just as seriously with issues involved in the *translation* of key documents that affect this same trade. If they don't address these issues, their companies may see their position in the international marketplace erode and their overall financial status threatened.

Among the principal issues that executives must consider in dealing with translations are:

1. What documents actually need to be translated?

2. Who should do the original translations?

3. How should these translations be checked?

4. How should disagreements in two different translations of the same document be resolved?

5. How much should a translation cost and how long should it take?

COMMERCIAL TRANSLATIONS

Each of these issues and a few others are discussed in some detail in the chapter that follows.

One final note here: The selection of a translation service should be a company decision, made with the same care and concern as the selection of an outside law or accounting firm. Often, however, the decision on translations is left to individual project managers or department chiefs.

Sometimes two or three different translation firms can be engaged simultaneously by the same company – leaving foreign sales people, suppliers, agents, and customers confused by the sometimes substantial differences *they* will note in the material received from what is ostensibly the same source.

In short, the benefits of familiarity with terminology and consistency of style – developed as the relationship between a company and a translation service grows and endures – cannot be overestimated.

THE
PRINCIPAL
ISSUES
OF
TRANSLATIONS

A sampling of the wide variety of documents requiring translation to maintain commercial competitiveness in world markets.
[Gregrey Harris Photography]

THE PRINCIPAL ISSUES OF TRANSLATIONS

The translation of any document from one language to another seems, on the surface, to be a fairly straightforward undertaking. Unfortunately, it seldom is.

At the outset, a choice has to be made about which documents need to be translated and the level of translation each may require. Some documents take considerably more care in translating than others.

The next step involves the choice of an appropriate translator. To find a person equally knowledgeable of how languages are used in two different countries can prove an exacting task.

It may not be enough to know French and English today. A translator may have to know how the French of Martinique should be translated to the English of Singapore. That same translator also has to have a sound knowledge of the subject matter of the document being translated in order to do an accurate job.

More often than not, a translator finds several plausible ways to render the crucial passages of a document from one language to another. Selecting the best equivalency is often the subject of intense debate among several linguists.

COMMERCIAL TRANSLATIONS

Were the decision between different words advocated by two linguists a matter of black and white, right and wrong, resolution of these debates would be swift. But languages tend to have unlimited subtlety and complexity. It can take as much diplomacy and psychology to settle a linguistic argument among translators as a domestic dispute between husband and wife.

The successful translation of any commercial document also relates to considerations of the cost and time involved. These can be as crucial to a business strategy as any of the other details of buying or selling a product or service.

The discussion of the principal issues involved in commercial translation in this chapter is designed to help readers obtain accurate translations of important documents at a reasonable cost within a given period of time.

1.
What Documents
Actually Need
To Be Translated?

As a general rule, any document ought to be translated if it has the potential to affect significantly the financial standing, legal position, safety performance, or equipment operations of a company involved in international commerce.

In Marco Polo's day, international commerce was universally conducted in a stylized language called Trade Farsi. Subsequently, other tongues became the dominant language of international commerce – Italian, Portuguese, Spanish, and then English.

By the time of World War II, most business transactions were conducted in one of 4 or 5 languages. Many of the individuals involved in foreign trade in those days were fluent enough to handle two or more of these languages simultaneously.

Today the range of languages used in commerce is considerably broader, the specialized vocabularies of each is greatly increased, and the number of people involved in the production of any single product or service significantly expanded.

> The second most spoken language in the world today is Hindi – some 9% of the world's population speaks it.

It is, of course, the native tongue of the vast majority of people living in India. While English is taught in the schools and is almost universally used in the commerce of the country, Hindi is the dominant language of everyday life.

That fact leads to a speculative question concerning the leak of methyl isocyanate into the atmosphere around the Union Carbide Corporation's plant in Bhopal, India. Some 2500 people died and more than 200,000 are estimated to have been injured in that December 1984 accident.

Could the damage from this tragedy have been at least containable – or perhaps even preventable – had company instruction manuals, safety procedures, and public signs been translated from English into Hindi?

The answer to this question is not now available and may never be. All that can be done, at this stage of the various investigations and court proceedings, is to speculate that even those individuals with advanced skills in another language often find themselves reverting to their native tongues in moments of extreme crisis, personal emotion, or deep introspection.

Besides safety, another area that requires mandatory translations involves legal and financial matters. Any document used in international trade that may have a potentially significant monetary impact on its recipients ought to be translated into the native tongues of those who must take action based on that document.

Obviously, buy/sell contracts fall into this realm, but so do many other arrangements that may involve a future financial liability on either party. Look at this example:

> In the 1970s, an American limited partnership undertook to explore for oil in the State of Israel. The partnership was to receive a royalty based on the value of any oil that was subsequently found and recovered.
>
> When oil was eventually produced in a field the partnership had explored, Israeli officials established the value of the production in terms of Israel's average daily *buying price of oil* from all of its sources.
>
> The Americans countered by saying that the value of the Israeli-produced oil – for purposes of the royalty calculation – was intended to be the average world *selling price* on the day the oil was recovered. Over time, the difference between Israel's often concessionary buying price and the free market world selling price amounted to millions of dollars.
>
> The matter went to an international arbitration panel for resolution. Some observers suggest that had the original exploration agreement been translated from English to Hebrew and back again into English, the matter might never have reached the dispute stage. These observers feel that the translation process would have exposed the ambiguity of how the valuation was to be calculated.

COMMERCIAL TRANSLATIONS

We hold that formal commitments involving important financial undertakings ought to be translated for the protection of all parties and in the interest of sound business practice.

Translations should also be ordered for any literature that supports or accompanies a product sold in different linguistic markets – whether a consumer item or an industrial tool. A better informed buyer is likely to get more benefit and longer performance from such products.

To this end, many manufacturers have learned to involve their graphic designers and translators in the early stages of creating product literature. While a picture or diagram usually serves all language versions, the length of the text may vary considerably depending on the language involved.

The following simple phrase illustrates the point:

THANK YOU FOR NOT SMOKING
[English]

U WORDT VERZOCHT NIET TE ROKEN
[Dutch]

WIR DANKEN FÜR DAS NICHTRAUCHEN
[German]

NOUS VOUS REMERCIONS DE NE PAS FUMER
[French]

TACK SKALL NI HA FÖR ATT NI INTE RÖKAR
[Swedish]

Multiple language versions of the same brochures, pamphlets, manuals and advertising copy can be printed more inexpensively if different texts are stripped into standard pages containing the same illustrations. With early and proper planning, this can readily be done.

The following examples illustrate the point that literature for products used abroad needs to be translated as consistently and as accurately as those affecting financial, legal, and safety matters.

- The managing director of a British forklift manufacturer believes that his use of one translation firm over the years has measureably enhanced his overseas business.

  His agents comment on the consistency of language style and standard nomenclature in all the printed material and advertising copy received. Importantly, this conveys to customers a sense of the company's stability and longevity in the marketplace.

- The Hewlett-Packard Company learned the same lesson last year. *The Wall St. Journal* reports that in a rush to translate a Spanish language manual for a new personal computer, the company divided the job among seven different translators.

  Among other things, they produced five different ways to say "disk drive." As a result, the company has now taken steps to consolidate and unify its translation work.

2.
Who Should Do
the
Original Translations?

The responsibility for translation generally rests with the party who generates the original documents involved in the purchase or sale of goods or services in international trade.

Invariably, however, the translation process – if it is done at all – is ordered by the *recipient* of the original documents. Out of almost universal habit, the mutually understandable language of informal discussion becomes the language of any resulting formal agreement. It is the recipient of these agreements who usually reverts to a translation should the implications of some of the formal terms in the original language not be clearly understood.

Major problems can arise when the general rule is violated. The problems relate to the nature of all communication.

The recipient of a document is simply not as familiar with the nuances of style, specialized wording, or technical phrases involved in the drafting of the original. As a result, recipients may unintentionally make seemingly small, apparently insignificant, errors when translating a very formal document.

Historically scholars have found ample evidence of scribes unwittingly making errors in documents they were copying--misreading passages, inadvertently making spelling errors ("not" instead of "now"), missing words, etc. Translators involved with unfamiliar styles, working on new material, transcribing hand written documents, or harboring some ideological bias can sometimes suffer from these same lapses.

To illustrate the possibility for error, look at the following sentence:

What pen are you going to use?

When this sentence is translated into Arabic, it would look like this:

ما نوع القلم الذي سيستعمل ؟

But if it were inadvertently rendered by a translator as:-

ما نوع العلم الذي سيستعمل ؟

– there would be a substantial difference between the two versions. The latter sentence reads: What *flag* are you going to use?

Look at the words: القلم and العلم in the two sentences. The latter lacks the accent dots called a *nughdha*. Its appearance or disappearance alters the word "pen" to "flag."

It is just this type of error, though, that can often confound and confuse subsequent communication between two parties. In effect, the parties may end up trying to resolve problems that have arisen only because they are working from what amounts to two different documents.

We recently came across an interesting illustration of the grief that ensues when drafters fail to do the original translation work:

COMMERCIAL TRANSLATIONS

An American airline, seeking to improve its market share on routes to and from Brazil, began a heavy advertising campaign announcing that it was installing "rendezvous lounges" on all of its flights.

It assumed that it had found a perfectly understandable and innocuous concept.

Had the airline done its own translations, however, it would have realized that the anglicized French word, "rendezvous," means something quite different in Portuguese. In fact, the word connotes a place for sex.

When Brazilian officials of the airline realized that they were expected to duplicate the advertising campaign in Portuguese, they insisted that their American colleagues scrap the program.

If nothing else, one assumes that they must have argued that proclaiming on-board "rendezvous lounges" would amount to false advertising to their Brazilian customers!

The episode proved to be an embarrassing, frustrating, and expensive lesson on the need to do translations at the point of origin.

3.
How Should
a Translation
Be Checked?

As a general rule, no major commercial translation task should be accepted as a valid rendering of an original document until it has been independently verified.

Verification, when called for, usually involves a two-step process:

1. The original document is translated into the desired second language.

2. This translation is then retranslated into the original language by a different, professionally qualified linguist.

While no translation can be an exact replica of the original, this two-step process has been found to be one in which the closest possible understandable equivalency from one language into another can be accomplished.

In fact, most such dual translations result in 95% agreement between the translators. The remaining 5% requires discussion to ensure absolute fidelity between the original document and the translation. These discussions usually revolve around the intended meaning of certain words and phrases.

The difficulty is well illustrated by a story about a college admissions officer who noted that prep school officials were complaining that their students were not being accepted in the numbers previously experienced.

"They think we're discriminating," the college officer is quoted as saying. "So do we, but we use the word in a different sense."

The need for verified translations is also demonstrated by the butchery some computer translation programs have done to common English expressions. Theodore Savory, in his book, *The Art of Translation,* reports on how one such computer program responded quite literally to its translating task:

Computer Translation	Original English
The whiskey is agreeable, but the meat has gone bad.	The spirit is willing, but the flesh is weak.
Invisible, imbecile.	Out of sight, out of mind.
Aquatic male sheep.	Hydraulic ram.

Computer translations are still perhaps 10 to 15 years away from common usage among commercial translation firms. While some major corporations are reported to be employing currently available foreign language computer programs for a first rough cut translation of certain kinds of material, most commercial translation firms feel these programs are not yet sophisticated enough to provide understandable translations for their clients. Nearly all computer translations now require a professional linguist to review and edit computer-produced copy for readability and accuracy.

Most commercial translation firms also find the cost of computer translation programs too high. At $11,000 to $50,000 per program – with each subject requiring a different program to encompass its specialized vocabulary – this technology offers little benefit in terms of the current workload of most commercial services.

In addition, many professional translators feel it is easier to create a translation from scratch rather than struggle to improve the syntax and usage that a computer may have rendered. An example was recently quoted in the journal, *The Incorporated Linguist*. A German to English machine translation provided the following:

> EDGAR NILL which we have quoted in our ARBEITSSCHUTZ-INFORMATIONEN already more often, a modern fable has devised in a contribution over risk-forecast. It/he warns to get across us against, in the reel of the big game hunter during/upon deployment of strategies for the improving the safety at work...

This same paragraph was then edited on a video display terminal by a professional linguist to read:

> EDGAR NILL, whom we have often quoted in our ARBEITSSCHUTZ-INFORMATIONEN, has devised a modern fable in a contribution about risk forecasting. When developing strategies for improving safety at work, he warns us against falling into the role of the big game hunter...

COMMERCIAL TRANSLATIONS

The overall conclusion of the author of the article is that "...a [computer's] logical system cannot be expected to have a human translator's *feel* for language...for all but the dryest and most factual of texts, results are so mediocre that editing is scarcely quicker than translating the text oneself in the first place..."

Computers are not the only translators that need checking. When the film "Chariots of Fire" was being prepared for re-recording onto video tape, a number of errors were found in the original Hebrew subtitles created for the film version.

For example, after the college dash scene, the Master says in English: "I doubt whether there is a swifter man in the Kingdom." When rendered originally into Hebrew for the film version, the same line read: "I doubt whether there is a sprinter in existence in the King's service."

The Sixth Commandment (Exodus 20:17) offers another illustration of how two separate translators – working in the same language combination – can choose different words to try to express what appears to be the same thought:

> "Thou Shalt Not Kill"
> [King James Version]

> "Thou Shalt Not Murder"
> [The Torah]

The verification process, had it been in use when the Bible was being translated into English, might have attempted to establish which of the words – "kill" or "murder" – was the correct translation from the original Hebrew.

In modern English, of course, the word "kill" is defined as depriving any living thing of life. The word "murder", on the other hand, refers much more narrowly to the unlawful killing of another human being.

It would appear from these definitions that murder is probably a more precise word today for the moral injunction of the Commandment. If kill were to be taken literally, man would be prohibited from slaughtering any animal or uprooting any plant for his sustenance.

There is a fourth example of how important verification can become. Jack Smith, a noted columnist for the *Los Angeles Times,* writes in his book, *The Pullet Surprise,* how one of his more innocent sentences caused considerable confusion among his readers.

The sentence in the column read:

> "A man chasing a cat with a broom in his underwear is ambience by any definition."

His readers responded with these types of comments:

- "Do you keep a broom in your underwear to solve a back problem?"

- "If you ever run into that cat with a broom in his underwear – grab your camera!"

- "I have known cats for many years, but have never seen one wearing underwear. Or outer wear, either, for that matter. Or was it you with the broom in your underwear?"

COMMERCIAL TRANSLATIONS

Jack Smith's sentence demonstrates how difficult it can be to establish an author's intended meaning. The point is that the verification procedures used in a translation task can generally expose even unintentional ambiguities and permit the original to be amended as required.

4.
How Are Differences
in Verified Translations
Resolved?

When substantive differences in meaning appear between the original document and its retranslation back to the first language, a formal review process to resolve the differences is required.

Most important commercial translation tasks today are no longer the work of a single individual laboring alone with a dictionary at his or her side. Rather, these translation tasks are team efforts that require discussion and sometimes independent research between at least two linguists working in the same combination of languages--whether Arabic/French, Japanese/Swedish, Russian/Spanish, or some other combination.

These linguistic partners generally develop substantive knowledge in the subject matter and vocabulary of one or more professional fields – law, medicine, the sciences, computers, art, economics, etc. Because technical knowledge has become highly refined, *The Directory of Translators and Translation Services* divides one scientific field – chemistry – into some seven defined *translation* specialities:

Analytical
Crystallography
Inorganic
Organic
Pharmaceutical
Physical
Radioisotope

COMMERCIAL TRANSLATIONS

Because of the specific vocabulary requirements of most scientific and technical fields, many major translation firms maintain large libraries of various dictionaries and reference books. Some have taken to preparing their own glossary of terms – in different languages – to help translate various specific technical matters or recurring words of art.

The expertise of two linguists, combined with a constantly up-dated knowledge of how any language is changing, generally promotes the basis for resolution of any translation differences:

> American teenagers in the 1970s began using the word "bad" to mean "very good" in much the same way that 18th century English speakers used the word "awful" – originally connoting something admirable or grand – to mean "terrible."

> The ironic tone employed with both words gave listeners the clue that the words were actually being used to convey something opposite from their traditional meanings.

> As "awful" came to imply something dreadful, so "bad" may come to be used often enough in the sense of "good" to change its basic meaning.

Two independent translators working on the same document from two different linguistic perspectives can generally spot and resolve these kinds of potentially subtle differences in usage.

Take another example. The following excerpts come from a press release promoting a San Francisco tour operation among European travelers:

CREATIVE SIGHTSEEING TOURS
SAVES THE BALLGAME
AS GRAYLINE STRIKES OUT

"San Francisco, April, 1984 – Creative Sightseeing Tours was founded by a former Grayline driver, now 'striking out on his own', and providing a whole new ballgame.

"We're covering all the bases ... the only tour company taking visitors where *they* want to go.

"Aside from its 'home' runs, Creative Sightseeing tours has made a lot of hits with its extension tours to Marin, the Wine Country, Tahoe, and Los Angeles."

The baseball analogies and Americanisms used in the press release were probably unintelligible, even to most English-speaking Europeans. It is also likely that they would not be recreated in any retranslation from an original foreign language translation.

But that is usually unimportant in commercial translation work. It is the precision of the *meaning* of the words, not the words themselves, that counts. As a result, the equivalents of these expressions, in the context of the document being translated, can readily be determined when the original is compared to the retranslation by two different specialists.

In some technical translations, third parties are brought in to analyze the translation/retranslation results. The third party helps to resolve any specific questions of interpretation.

More importantly, third parties can determine not only whether the resulting effort conveys the original meaning, but also whether the finished translation is readable and intelligible to the individual who will see only the translation itself.

5.
How Much Should
a Translation Cost
and How Long Should
It Take?

As a rule of thumb, a straight-forward translation should cost, at 1985 prices, in the neighborhood of 10¢ per word.

The rule of thumb, however, is often ignored. About a year ago, we asked 5 different American translation services to bid on the cost of converting a 1200-word capabilities brochure from its original English to Arabic, Swedish, French, German, and Spanish.

Because we knew that the cost of translations can often be dictated by time constraints, formatting requirements, delivery modes, and assorted other administrative factors, we made our request very simple. We specified that we would need the translation in about 45 days, that a straight typescript would be adequate, and that any inquiries during the translation process could be made by collect telephone call.

The results were staggering. We received bids ranging from $145 for an English to French text to $1200 for the English to German version.
One bid was provided in a casual telephone call, a few firms wrote letters, and one completed its own elaborate bidding forms specifying everything from paper size to margin widths.

We concluded from this survey that the vast differences in cost among translation services may be based only on what each thinks the buyer can afford.

COMMERCIAL TRANSLATIONS

Translation work in the United States still seems small and localized enough to withstand the leveling pressures that broad-based competition usually prompts. Quite obviously, translation jobs are not yet as prevalent as construction projects where nationwide bidding procedures tend to force cost estimates into a fairly narrow range.

The enormous variation in pricing may change as awareness of what is wanted and required in a translation task increases among purchasing agents, legal staffs, administrative personnel, and other business people responsible for assigning this type of work.

Elsewhere, competition among translation services seems stronger. A European Economic Community survey published in 1984 has estimated the average current cost of a translation at $8 per 100 words. Most typewritten pages, the survey notes, carry 250 words (+/− 10%).

But the average cost of a translation job is just that − an average. Actual pricing will be dependent upon a number of specific factors that buyers will want to consider:

> • Longer documents tend to have a significantly lower per word price than shorter ones. Firms like longer projects because administrative costs shrink sharply while the productivity of their salaried staff increases markedly.
>
> In addition, most firms set a minimum charge for very short documents such as birth certificates or school diplomas. The current minimum charge seems to be around $25 to $30.

- Esoteric topics, highly technical matters, and exotic languages tend to be more costly than standard subject matter or popular languages.

  Competent translators and editors in narrow fields or little known languages are obviously harder to find and can therefore command higher fees.

- The usage of the finished translation often has a bearing on the estimated price. A technical article from a foreign journal to be reviewed for its content requires a lesser degree of precision than a final contract committing two parties to a formal relationship.

  Advertising copy or an instruction manual typeset in a foreign language for immediate publication also might require a linguistic copywriter as well as a competent translator.

But for purposes of budgeting and bid comparison, 10¢ per word for a professional commercial translation of 250 words or more in any Western European language is a reasonable 1985 standard in the United States.

Corporate executives should be prepared, however, for a 15¢ per word average charge when translated material is being prepared for formal publication and as much as 20¢ per word when legal documents are involved.

The doubling in average price for legal work is perhaps best explained by *The Tulsa Tribune's* well-known 1959 description of legal language:

"When a man gives you an orange, he simply says: 'Have an orange.' But when the transaction is entrusted to a lawyer, he adopts this form: 'I hereby give and convey to you, all and singular, my estate and interest, right, title, claim and advantages of and in said orange, together with its rind, skin, juice, pulp, and pips and all rights and advantages therein and full power to bite, suck, or otherwise eat the same or give the same away with or without the rind, skin, juice, pulp and pips...' "

Not only is a legal vocabulary more precise, but each word has to be assessed for its correct meaning. It obviously produces much longer documents as well.

Most translation services assume that a translator can work at a steady pace of between 300 and 500 words – or 1¼ to 2 pages – per hour. Their actual speed will depend on the nature of the material being translated, the methodology employed in making the translation, and the formatting requirements of the document.

Companies should also be aware of other factors when gauging the length of time any particular job will take:

- Advance notice to a translation firm of the dimensions of a pending task will permit the firm to plan its personnel commitments to ensure that the most qualified translators are available when needed.

- The longer the period of time that can be allowed to complete a translation task, the more likely that the firm will have an adequate period for reflection, consultation, research, and revision.

In most cases, it is better to get a translation service started on a portion of a document than to wait for the entire project to be completed. Any questions of style, vocabulary, nomenclature, formatting, or other matters can be resolved that much earlier and hasten the ultimate completion of the entire job.

6.
Other Translation Issues

There are, of course, other translation issues that may have to be addressed by larger firms. For example:

- When should an in-house translation capability be developed in total or partial substitution for contractor services?

- When is it safe – because of morale or status considerations – to allow an on-the-scene agent or distributor to translate documents as opposed to a professional translator?

While these are questions involving answers well beyond the scope of this present effort, a few comments are in order. In-house translators often fulfill the same role as in-house lawyers. Both tend to do routine matters and handle internal needs in their respective fields.

When highly specialized work arises or when workload factors require additional manpower, they engage and supervise outside firms. In-house lawyers, for example, might use outside counsel for tax or litigation work. In-house translators, on the other hand, might use an outside translation firm to produce foreign language versions of operating manuals or bidding documents.

Problems, of course, can arise – particularly in the area of verification and editing – with in-house translators. An example comes to mind:

An English consulting firm, engaged to study the safety and efficiency of power plants all over the world, employed one man for 15 years as its French translator.

When that translator wanted additional work in his spare time, the examining panel of a translation firm had to reject him for substandard ability.

His employer – unable to speak French – never knew that this long-standing translator had severe problems with the language he was employed to translate.

We suggest that when more complex translation-related issues arise, a competent management consultant skilled in international administrative practices be engaged to advise on the matter.

The questions that help resolve the principal issues discussed above – what documents should be translated, who should do the original translation, how to check translations differences, and the cost and timing of translations – are dealt with in detail in the following chapter.

COMMERCIAL TRANSLATIONS

A
CHECKLIST
FOR
CHOOSING
A
PROFESSIONAL
TRANSLATION
SERVICE

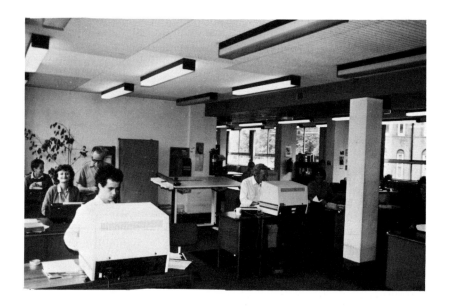

A view of some of the personnel, equipment and reference material used by a major full-service translation firm today.
[Henry Mendes Photography]

A CHECKLIST FOR CHOOSING
A PROFESSIONAL
TRANSLATION SERVICE

There is no accurate count of the number of translation firms now operating in the United States. This industry, like so many others, is not subject to any formal licensing procedures or educational qualifications.

Any person with self-evaluated bilingual capability can rent a phone line, drop a name into a classified directory, or declare himself or herself to be a professional translator ready for business. Because of this, reliance on the size or prominance of a yellow page ad – as a gauge of competence – can prove to be erroneous.

Of course, some freelance and part-time individuals may be very competent and very talented translators. In some language combinations or subject fields, they may be the only ones readily available.

But knowing the difference between freelance and part-time translators only describes part of the structure of the translation business. Some of these translators deal exclusively with their own clientele while others are linked indirectly to the client through a translation agency – firms that actively seek and distribute translation work.

For the most part, translation agencies act as brokers for independent translators. As such, agencies are not likely to have any linguists on their staff. Other than managerial and administrative personnel, translation agencies generally lack the capability or the resources to verify or edit material produced by their outside contractors.

COMMERCIAL TRANSLATIONS

Because agencies work on fixed margins added to the fees charged by their contracting translators, the agencies usually cannot afford to pay for independent verification of the accuracy or quality of every item translated. The danger, of course, is that some of this work may turn out to be shoddy.

In our view, better work is likely to arise from full-time translators employed by full-service translation firms. These translators tend to be more familiar with current business usage, have better equipment and facilities at hand, and always have professional verification or editorial talent available to review their work.

While even full-service translation firms must engage outside independent translators from time to time – because of workload factors, language requirements, or specialized projects – the work of these outsiders is still subject to the same verification and editorial procedures used with on-staff personnel.

With this structural background in mind, firms in international commerce need a checklist of prime and follow-on questions to ask any translator or translation firm before settling on a particular individual or company to do any job at hand.

The most often asked questions of translation firms revolve around the following four areas of concern:

I   The languages handled by the firm's linguists.

II   The price to translate a given document.

III   The length of time to deliver the completed translation.

IV   The firm's fields of specialty and experience in translation work.

We have looked at each of these areas of concern in terms of the major and subordinate questions that ought to be asked to qualify a firm for a particular task or to determine if a long term relationship would be appropriate.

In addition, there are a number of questions that are seldom asked, but ought to be. We have grouped these under two additional categories:

V   The verification and editing procedures employed by the translation firm.

VI   The administrative practices of the translation firm.

Not all the principal questions or supplemental enquiries, of course, need to be asked. Answers to some will obviate the necessity of posing others. Taken together, though, the responses to the full list will represent a comprehensive statement about the capability of any translator or translation firm.

We have also grouped the 22 principal questions together at the end of the chapter in two ways to facilitate their review:

1.   In the precise order in which we have presented them within the six categories.

2.   In an order that might be used in addressing them to a translation firm.

In addition, we have added a list of the five most important points to be covered when formally authorizing a translator's work or seeking a cost estimate.

I
QUESTIONS
PERTAINING TO
LANGUAGES HANDLED.

☐   **How did the designated translator(s) learn the language combination involved?**

• At home/At home?

• At home/At school?

• At school/At school?

• At home/Through living experience?

• At school/Through living experience?

• Through living experience/Through living experience?

One of the rules used by most responsible translation firms is that a translator must translate *into* his native tongue and that at least one of his languages must have been refined through some kind of formal education.

If a computer is used as the initial translator, please see pages 47-49 and page 84 for comments.

☐ **What kind of additional credentials will the translator assigned to the task bring to his or her work?**

• Education/Publications?

• Other work experience/honors/degrees?

• Years (   ) of experience as a professional translator in the subject field?

• Membership in professional organizations?

A translator's collateral skills in one or more subject fields or technical areas should significantly enhance the accuracy and quality of a translation.

☐ **How does the designated translator(s) keep current with language changes in the two languages in which he or she will be working?**

Speaks both languages in the combination at home or consistently with relatives and friends?

Subscribes and/or reads periodicals and books in both languages?

Travels frequently to native country or other areas where the language is spoken?

Does work other than translating requiring a facility in both languages?

Translators are like any other professional: If they fail to keep up with changes in language and usage, their resulting translations will likely sound stilted to, or be misunderstood by, the reader.

The more a translator is involved in each of the four follow-on questions, the better work he or she is likely to produce.

In addition to keeping abreast of changes in their native tongue(s), we believe translators must also be interested in keeping up with the changes and nuances of their adopted language as well.

☐   **Will translator(s) assigned to this task be available for questions on meaning or interpretation of phrases after delivery of the finished work?**

Will there be an added charge for this aspect of the service?

Is the translator a competent *interpreter* in the event that the foreign recipients want to discuss the translation in depth directly with company officials? (For a discussion of the difference between translating and interpreting, see pages 93 to 94.)

If, after discussion, a more accurate way to phrase something is agreed to , will the service provide freshly typed copies for delivery to others?

In all cases, the answer to the basic question ought to be yes. The only exception that comes to mind is when a translator has a scheduling conflict.

A CHECKLIST FOR CHOOSING A PROFESSIONAL TRANSLATION SERVICE

II
QUESTIONS
PERTAINING TO THE
PRICE OF TRANSLATING

☐ **How much will the translation cost?**

• Is this a total cost or are there add-ons?

• What other costs might be incurred?

      – For overtime?

      – For telephone charges?

      – For extra copies?

      – For proof-reading typeset text?

      – For third party consultation with translator?

      – For delivery surcharge?

See pages 56-60 for a detailed discussion on the issue of cost.

Handwritten or photocopied material submitted for translation is sometimes difficult to read. Some firms will charge extra if partially illegible documents create unusual problems.

There is one other point. Some firms agree to rebate a portion of their fee as a penalty for failure to meet a fixed deadline for completion, particularly when a premium has been paid for overtime work. It is worth asking whether a firm under consideration has such a policy.

☐ **How long will the price quotation given for a translation remain valid?**

• Does the translation firm have other pressures in this language combination at this time?

• Can an option fee be paid to hold the quotation firm beyond a usual 30 days?

☐ **What are the normal terms for payment?**

• Is a deposit required?

• If so, is the full amount due on completion?

• Can payment of the balance be made within 30 days of completion?

As with other service businesses, these matters are usually governed by local business practice. They should, however, be discussed between the translator and the client to avoid misunderstanding.

III
QUESTIONS
PERTAINING TO
TIMING

☐ **How long will the translation take?**

• Can payment be made for a faster turn-around time?

• Will the service work overtime if necessary to meet a deadline?

• Can chapters and/or sections be delivered as they are completed?

See pages 59-60 for a discussion of timing issues.

The basic axiom of translation timing is that the more lead time given and the longer the period of time allowed to complete a job, the better the work and the lower the ultimate costs.

Length of time estimates are usually based on the availability of specific translators for certain jobs. As a result, companies may want to enquire about how long a time estimate will remain valid.

Verification and editing requirements add further time to a translation task. In addition, many high technology and consumer firms leave extra time for testing a foreign translation with sample users prior to the final publication of a document.

☐ **Can copy be submitted in parts, and can the translation service handle last-minute changes?**

Documents to be submitted under fixed deadlines are often subject to continuous alteration by their originators. Some services are used to this kind of work; most, however, do not have sufficient staff to deal with the pressure involved.

Part-time translators sometimes have the most difficulty in handling constant revisions and last – minute demands. Readers may wish to review Scene V in the Foreword for an illustration of the kinds of problems that can arise when part-time translators are engaged on deadline projects.

☐ **How will the translated document be delivered?**

• By courier?

• By telex?

A CHECKLIST FOR CHOOSING A PROFESSIONAL TRANSLATION SERVICE

• By facsimile machine?

• By mail?

Most full-service translation firms are equipped to deliver material to their clients by any of these methods; part-time translators may not be.

IV
QUESTIONS
PERTAINING TO
TRANSLATING EXPERIENCE

☐ **Has the translator/service worked in this area of specialty before?**

• When?

• For whom? (This information, however, may be confidential.)

• What kind of documents were translated?

The more direct experience a translator has with a particular subject field or in a specialized technical area, the more likely his or her work will be responsive to a given translation need. A translator concentrating on scripts for television commercials may not be as accurate or as precise when translating a proposal for building a port facility.

Because of the enormous number of highly specialized subjects that even the largest firms can be called upon to translate, companies can increase the accuracy and speed of the work done for them by supplying the translation firm with

with reference material, copies of previous translations, foreign language articles on the subject, and the like.

Please see Scene I in the Foreword to understand better the benefit of establishing a relationship with a translation firm staffed to handle a wide variety of languages.

☐ **Will the translation task be assigned to a full-time employee or part-time contractor?**

Many translation services have only one or two on-staff people. We believe translators who work only occasionally can become rusty in both language usage and efficiency.

Readers may wish to reread Scenes II and III in the Foreword to get a sense of the kind of problems that can occur when part-time translators are engaged on commercial work.

V
QUESTIONS
PERTAINING TO
VERIFICATION/
EDITING

☐ **What verification/editing procedures are employed to ensure accuracy and readability?**

• Work done by one translator is checked by an equally qualified second translator?

• All translations are done by two independent translators working separately?

• Translations are checked by an editor?

• Competent third party verifiers are available when required?

We recommend that some independent verification/ editing process be employed in each translation task. We prefer the option expressed in the first follow-on question, because it is usually less expensive than the second option.

Editing is sufficient for certain less complex or technical subjects, but competent third party verifiers should always be available.

To facilitate editing, companies should convert any measurement notations and/or foreign currency amounts they wish included before submitting a document for translation.

Scene VI in the Foreword suggests a typical problem when strong verification/editing procedures are not employed by a translation service.

☐ **Will the completed translation be formally certified as to its accuracy?**

• For legal/judicial review?

• For governmental purposes?

Formal certification of a translation is sometimes required. Be sure that the exact nature of the certification is ascertained before enquiring if the translator has the proper credentials to provide it.

In addition, if the translator is required to swear to the accuracy of his or her translation before a foreign consular official or in a legal proceeding, extra time and costs may be involved.

VI
QUESTIONS
PERTAINING TO
ADMINISTRATIVE
PRACTICES

☐ **How many copies of the translation work are normally delivered with the original?**

• Can the service handle printing and binding of the copies?

• Can the service also handle typesetting and layouts in a foreign language?

Translation firms that provide a broad range of support services obviously increase the efficiency of clients in meeting their responsibility to deliver a finished product on time.

☐ **Estimate the amount of space (number of lines or pages) that translation will involve?**

Many languages, as noted on page 41, take more space than English to convey the same meaning. While a seemingly unimportant question, the length of a translation may have a bearing on delivery decisions, formatting choices, binding material, literature design, and other matters.

A CHECKLIST FOR CHOOSING A PROFESSIONAL TRANSLATION SERVICE

A story recently reported in Computer World *tells how one firm failed to leave sufficient room on its software program for responses to its procedural prompts. Every time German-speaking users tried to insert the appropriate command in their native language, the system collapsed.*

☐ **How will the finished product be formatted?**

• Straight typewritten text?

• Will follow format of original to the extent possible?

The choice of formats should be given to the client, not assumed by the translation service. In certain kinds of documents – scripts, flyers, advertisements – formatting may determine a reader's understanding of, and reaction to, the material.

If handwritten material is submitted, the format of the translation should be discussed with the translator before he or she begins work.

Finally, if the finished copy is to be sent out on company stationery or other specially printed material, it is better to provide the blank stock to the translation service. This avoids the chance of error when a translation is recopied on an improperly equipped machine or by a non-native-speaking typist.

☐ **What technique will be used by the translator in preparing the translation?**

• Dictates translation to a recording device or a secretary as he or she reads the original?

• Produces first draft on a typewriter?

• Produces work on a word processor?

• Material is first translated by computer before editing by a professional linguist?

We believe the most efficient method – the fastest overall and least prone to error – is a translator dictating into a machine for transcription into the typist's mother tongue.

Translators who use word processors, work in longhand, or set out text on typewriters are generally less efficient in getting the complete job done.

A CHECKLIST FOR CHOOSING A PROFESSIONAL TRANSLATION SERVICE

Computer translations are generally not yet acceptable unless they are completely and carefully edited by a professional linguist. See the discussion on pages 47-49.

☐ **Will the original be returned with the translation?**

- Will the translator/service retain a copy of the original document?

- Does the translation service keep a hard copy or disk of the completed translation?

Copies should be retained by the service in the event of questions or follow-on work. In the latter case, costs can be reduced if the translation task involves revision of work previously completed.

If, however, the client requests that the original be returned, with all copies destroyed and/or disks erased, the translation service should comply with the request without hesitation.

☐ **What assurances can be given that no one associated with the translator/service will use information derived from the original without the expressed written consent of the client?**

- Are staff members bound to a rule of confidentiality in their employment contracts or during hiring procedures?

• What security procedures are used to safeguard the original and translation from unauthorized disclosure?

We believe that translators must care for client material as carefully as they care for their own.

☐ **Who will own the copyright on the translation when completed?**

In most literary translations, the translator owns the copyright on his or her work. In business translations, translators should acquire no rights to the finished product and should not use any of the material translated for an ancillary purpose.

☐ **Does the translator/service carry professional liability insurance?**

• Has the translator/service ever been involved in a lawsuit pertaining to the unauthorized disclosure of information derived from a translation task?

• Has any other lawsuit been filed or decided that reflects on the skills, commitments, or work of the firm?

The Association of Translation Companies in the United Kingdom requires that its member firms carry professional liability coverage.

A CHECKLIST FOR CHOOSING A PROFESSIONAL TRANSLATION SERVICE

We believe this type of insurance offers clients of translation firms important financial protection in the event that an error in translation requires a document to be reprinted, contributes to an industrial accident, or causes some other cost to be borne by the client company.

There is another reason why companies ought to ask translation firms about their liability coverage. If they have it, their record for accuracy is probably fairly high. If they don't, they may be too small or too financially insecure, or they may have even been rejected or dropped by a liability carrier in the past.

CHECKLIST
IN ORDER OF PRESENTATION

*To make our checklist of questions
easier for readers to review, we have
repeated the principal questions below
in the order in which they were
presented.*

1. How did the designated translator(s) learn the language combination involved?

2. What kind of additional credentials will the translator assigned to the task bring to his or her work?

3. How does the designated translator(s) keep current with language changes in the two languages in which he or she will be working?

4. Will translator(s) assigned to this task be available for questions on meaning or interpretation of phrases after delivery of the finished work?

5. How much will the translation cost?

6. How long will the price quotation given for a translation remain valid?

7. What are the normal terms for payment?

8. How long will the translation take?

A CHECKLIST FOR CHOOSING A PROFESSIONAL TRANSLATION SERVICE

9. Can copy be submitted in parts, and can the translation service handle last-minute changes?

10. How will the translated document be delivered?

11. Has the translator/service worked in this area of speciality before?

12. Will the translation task be assigned to a full-time employee or part-time contractor?

13. What verification/editing procedures are employed to ensure accuracy and readability?

14. Will the completed translation be formally certified as to its accuracy?

15. How many copies of the translation work are normally delivered with the original?

16. Estimate the amount of space (number of lines or pages) that the translation will involve?

17. How will the finished product be formatted?

18. What technique will be used by the translator in preparing the translation?

19. Will the original be returned with the translation?

20. What assurances can be given that no one associated with the translator/service will use information derived from the original without the expressed written consent of the client?

21. Who will own the copyright on the translation when completed?

22. Does the translator/service carry professional liability insurance?

CHECKLIST
IN PRIORITY ORDER

We have arranged the 22 questions below in the priority in which they might be asked of a translation firm.

1. How long will the translation take?

2. Has the translator/service worked in this area of speciality before?

3. Will the translation task be assigned to a full-time employee or part-time contractor?

4. How did the designated translator(s) learn the language combination involved?

5. What kinds of additional credentials will the translator assigned to the task bring to his or her work?

6. Will the translator(s) assigned to this task be available for questions on meaning or interpretation of phrases after delivery of the finished work?

7. How much will the translation cost?

8. How long will the price quotation given for a translation remain valid?

9. Can copy be submitted in parts, and can the translation service handle last-minute changes?

10. What verification/editing procedures are employed to ensure accuracy and readability?

A CHECKLIST FOR CHOOSING A PROFESSIONAL TRANSLATION SERVICE

11. Will the completed translation be formally certified as to its accuracy?

12. How does the designated translator(s) keep current with language changes in the two languages in which he or she will be working?

13. How will the translated document be delivered?

14. How many copies of the translation work are normally delivered with the original?

15. Estimate the amount of space (number of lines or pages) that the translation will involve?

16. How will the finished product be formatted?

17. What technique will be used by the translator in preparing the translation?

18. What are the normal terms for payment?

19. Will the original be returned with the translation?

20. Does the translator/service carry professional liability insurance?

21. What assurances can be given that no one associated with the translator/service will use information derived from the original without the expressed written consent of the client?

22. Who will own the copyright on the translation when completed?

TRANSLATION INSTRUCTIONS

Once a translation service has been selected, companies should cover the following points in their purchase orders, letter agreements, or verbal commitments when authorizing a particular translation job or when seeking a formal cost estimate.

1. Specify the *language* or *languages* into which the original is to be translated, as well as the country or countries where the translation will be used.

2. Indicate the *purpose* of the translation – whether it will be used for information, publication, legal, or other ends.

3. Provide the *date* the translation will be required and the means of delivery preferred.

4. Specify the *format* requirements for the final translated copy or provide a sample of how the material should look.

5. State any additional *services* – extra originals, number of copies, typesetting, long-term storage of material for future revisions – that may be required.

SOME CONCLUDING THOUGHTS ABOUT COMMERCIAL TRANSLATIONS

Interpretation booths overlooking the UN general assembly rostrum illustrates the importance of this linguistic specialty to international communication.

[United Nations Photo]

SOME CONCLUDING THOUGHTS
ABOUT COMMERCIAL
TRANSLATIONS

A word needs to be said about how the role of the *interpreter* differs from that of a translator. Although these are closely allied professions, they have become specialized into two separate areas of expertise.

Both, of course, are committed to the goal of providing understandable communication as if no language barrier existed. Interpreters must try to achieve this goal instantaneously – as an individual is speaking.

Translators, on the other hand, have the comparative luxury of writing and rewriting phrases or sections until the translated meaning is as close to the original as possible. Some also have acquired extensive libraries of reference books, dictionaries, and other material to assist them in understanding the original and developing the best equivalency in another language.

But written communication is static. Translators receive no assistance in conveying meaning from a raised eyebrow, a chuckle, or a change in tone of voice. Interpreters sometimes do.

Translators try to express the written thoughts of others in the most exact and appropriate equivalent terms available; interpreters are expected to be absolutely literal – speaking instantaneously without any embellishment, omission, or editing.

COMMERCIAL TRANSLATIONS

William M. O'Barr in his book *Linguistic Evidence* makes the point that one simple thought, when verbally expressed by four different people, can indicate important information about each speaker:

> • "I don't got no job."
> *This suggests a speaker whose native language, like Spanish, may require double negatives.*

> • "Job, I don't have one."
> *The syntax sometimes used in English by a German or Yiddish speaker.*

> • "I ain't got no job."
> *A dialectical word usage common among some Americans.*

> • "I don't have a job."
> *Generally considered to be Standard American English*

The broader information clues provided by syntax and grammar in verbal expression would, in all probability, disappear in the course of completing a commercial translation.

Because interpreters are required to be literal, the Los Angeles Superior Court system has created a dictionary of terms to assist interpreters in handling slang-laced speech often used by witnesses. As an example, some 15 colloquial words used to discuss marijuana and dozens more to describe sexual matters are listed. While a translator might clean up language to aid comprehension or to avoid misunderstanding, interpreters do not.

The conclusion is that just as a good writer may be a horrendous bore when lecturing, so outstanding interpreters may make poor translators. Conversely, of course, we know of many excellent translators who are inadequate as interpreters. Under pressure, they literally can become tongue-tied.

SOME CONCLUDING THOUGHTS ABOUT COMMERCIAL TRANSLATIONS

Translating, quite clearly, is a separate and unique scholarly skill. We believe it to be an extremely important one in the successful conduct of international business today.

Boris Pasternak, perhaps, best expresses the goal of all who practice this special art:

> "I believe, as do many others, that closeness to the original is not ensured only by literal exactness or by similarity of form: the likeness, as in a portrait, cannot be achieved without a lively and natural method of expression. Like the original, the translation must create an impression of life and not of verbiage."

Pasternak's words first appeared in 1956 in an essay called "Translating Shakespeare." Pasternak's thoughts on translations, interestingly enough, are only available to us through the skill of his translator, Manya Harari.

But that, we think, has been the whole point of this book. Translation, as an art, is perhaps as old as written literature itself. It is an integral part of our need to communicate and understand each other.

There is no doubt that without the efforts of translators, our lives would not be as rich; with translators, mankind has the ability to expand its potential beyond the restrictions imposed by linguistic boundaries.

COMMERCIAL TRANSLATIONS

POSTSCRIPT

COMMERCIAL TRANSLATIONS

POSTSCRIPT

Both of the authors of this book are currently involved in commercial translation work, one to a much greater extend than the other. About a year ago, we sensed the need to try to develop a simple checklist to help company executives select the most qualified individuals or firms for the translation tasks these officials are increasingly called upon to authorize.

But as so often happens with projects of this nature, a simple start turned into a much more complex undertaking. Each item on our blossoming checklist seemed to warrant an explanation and each explanation spawned examples to reinforce the points we wanted to make.

Before long, the project involved a search of the contemporary literature on translations, an informal survey of the pricing policies of American translation services, and a review of current commercial translation practices. In short, we had the makings of a brief book on our hands.

When we discovered that no comprehensive work on the subject of *commercial* translations had yet been published, we committed ourselves to the larger task of writing it. We hope the final result of our effort will have proven as worthwhile to readers as it was enlightening for us to prepare.

A brief word about the authors seems appropriate so that both our biases and our backgrounds are on record for the reader:

Godfrey Harris is president of Harris/Ragan Management Corporation, a public policy and management consulting firm based in Los Angeles, California.

After teaching political science at the University of California, Los Angeles, and at Rutgers University, he entered the U.S. Foreign Service.

As a diplomat, he soon learned that a facility to speak a foreign language in no way qualified him to write in a literate or accurate manner in that language. It was then that he began to appreciate the skills and talents of translators.

He has not, however, been as reticent in writing in English. Harris has previously written *The History of Sandy Hook* and *Panama's Position* and co-authored *The Quest for Foreign Affairs Officers*. In addition, he has published more than a dozen articles on various subjects.

Charles Sonabend is managing director of Transtelex Limited, a London-based, international translation firm.

He was born in Brussels of French-speaking parents and moved to England as a' young man. There he worked to perfect his spoken and written English prior to entering the London School of Economics.

Upon graduation, Sonabend began his successful business career as a Chartered Accountant (CPA). He later established a number of service companies that eventually led to his position at Transtelex.

He has built Transtelex into one of the most comprehensive translation services in the world with a large in-house staff of 30 professional linguists. It is a technologically advanced, centrally operated, international translation service.

His own facility in English and French – as well as in several other languages – is such that at times he has undertaken some of the more complex legal and financial verification responsibilities himself.

One final note: In drafting this book on commercial translations, we found ourselves faced with our *own* mini-translation problem – whether to write in American English or British English. Do we refer to bids as tenders, for example, or trucks as lorries? Do we spell in the American or English tradition – neighbors or neighbours, realize or realise?

After some debate, we decided that American business people, more than their British counterparts, need to increase their sensitivity to the decisions faced in selecting a translation firm. As a result, we decided on Americanisms to ease the learning burden for readers in the United States.

We therefore apologise to English readers who faced their own small translation hurdles in working through the material. We must also apologize to our family members, friends, and colleagues who were kind enough to review the manuscript for us, but whose thoughtful comments may have slipped our attention in the final editing process. The felicitious phrases and perfect words are theirs; the errors of commission and omission are ours.

COMMERCIAL TRANSLATIONS

Although we should thank everybody who helped us in some way to put this project together, we must extend a special thanks to our close associates – William Butler, Gregrey Harris, and Charles Jamieson – who gave so freely of their professional knowledge and time to assist us.

Godfrey Harris
Charles Sonabend

London
June, 1985

BIBLIOGRAPHICAL
NOTES

COMMERCIAL TRANSLATIONS

BIBLIOGRAPHICAL NOTES

Many of the data, stories, and examples referred to in this book have come from our own observations or from exchanges with our clients over the past 25 years.

Because of the proprietary nature of some of this material, we have tried to describe the circumstances and events of each accurately without specifically identifying the personalities or companies involved--either in the text itself or in the notes below.

We also reviewed some of the contemporary literature on translations and linguistics. For those interested – and to assure that proper credit is given to the work of others from whom we learned and benefited – we have added these informal biographical notes to identify more precisely the quoted matter in the text.

"SOME GENERAL THOUGHTS ON TRANSLATIONS"

p. 19   The biblical quotes were derived from bibles published by The World Publishing Company, New York (Authorized King James Version) and by Thomas Nelson & Sons (Revised Standard Edition, 1952.)

James A. Michener's book, *The Source* (Random House, Inc., 1965) contributed to our thinking on the way people think about and react to events.

Barry Hoberman's comprehensive article "Translating the Bible" in the February 1985 issue of *The Atlantic Monthly* was also rewarding reading.

p. 22   The Peter Glassgold phrase quoted appeared in an article he wrote for the May 18, 1984, edition of *Publishers Weekly*. A copy of the article was sent to us by PEN American Center. Their pamphlets – "The Responsibilities of Translators" and "A Translation Model Contract" – were also helpful in sharpening our thinking about the modern differences between literary and commercial translations.

We also found an interesting short history of translations in the 1984 edition of the *Americana Encyclopedia* by J.M. Cohen. It helped us put this scholarly field into perspective.

Our cultural examples were derived from a December 1984 article appearing in the *Los Angeles Times* on gift giving and a 1985 *Computer Weekly* piece called "Spreading the Word Abroad".

pp. 24-25   The collection of amateur translations we use appeared in "Lost in Translation," *The Saturday Evening Post,* September 1982.

p. 26   The excerpt from an environmental consultant's report was made available to us by a client of Harris/Ragan Management Corporation.

p. 27   The story about Pepsi Cola's translation problems in Taiwan was reported by the London *Evening Standard* in 1984.

"THE EXPLOSION OF LANGUAGES USED IN INTERNATIONAL COMMERCE"

pp. 31-34   The bulk of the language statistics was derived from *Better Translation for Better Communication* by Bureau Marcel van Dijk (Brussels) and PA Conseiller de Direction (Paris). The monograph was prepared in 1983 for the Commission of the European Communities and published by Pergamon Press.

In addition, we used the 1965 edition of *Translations and Translation Services and Sources in Science and Technology,* a publication of the Special Libraries Association, Frances E. Kaiser, editor.

Other facts for this segment were found in an article in the January 17, 1985, edition of "Computer Weekly" and from interviews with officials of the Department of State in Washington, D.C.

p. 35   The proportion of the U.S. gross national product dependent on foreign trade is charted in a U.S. Department of State report prepared by James Ragan Associates entitled: "Foreign Affairs Workload Indicators and Comparative Agency Resources," July 1982.

The paragraph written by a German businessman was taken verbatim from a letter received in December 1984 by a client of Harris/Ragan Management Corporation.

p. 36   The story describing how a Belgian firm lost a follow-on contract comes from an internal memorandum prepared by a staff member of Transtelex Limited.

pp. 37-38   The conversation with an English truck driver is quoted in an unpublished manuscript, written in 1965, by Godfrey Harris.

p. 38   The example of how content analysis affects advertising copy was found in a *Wall Street Journal* article called "Pollster Lets Interviewees Ramble on, Lets Computer Sift Answers for Key Words". The article appeared on February 13, 1985.

"THE PRINCIPAL ISSUES OF TRANSLATION"

p. 46   The facts used to describe the Union Carbide accident at Bhopal, India, were derived from many different news sources. We have seen published photographs of areas of the plant in which signs are in English only. (See for one, "Frightening Findings at Bhopal," *Time,* February 18, 1985.)

p. 47   The facts of the oil dispute in Israel were derived from proprietary sources.

p. 48   The phrase "Thank you for Not Smoking" is a slogan used by an English organization called ASH – Action on Smoking and Health. The translations into other languages were provided by staff members of Transtelex Limited.

p. 49   The forklift manufacturer is a client of Transtelex Limited.

                 The Hewlett-Packard 'Co. story appeared in a March 1985 *Wall Street Journal* article called "Computers Gain as Language Translators Even Though Perfect Not They Always."

pp. 50-51   The historical comments were derived, in part, from articles in *The Atlantic Monthly* and *Americana Encyclopedia,* mentioned above at p. 21 and p. 22.

p. 51   The Arabic example was provided by a translator on the staff of Transtelex Limited.

p. 52   The airline example was told in *The Saturday Evening Post* story described in these notes at pp. 24-25.

p. 54   The quotations from the college admissions officer were found in a *Wall Street Journal* article appearing on April 2, 1985.

                The computer translation samples appeared in Theodore Savory's, *The Art of Translation,* 1968, The Writer, Inc., p. 177. The *Wall Street Journal* article referenced at p. 49 above used some of the same examples and provided the cost data noted.

pp. 54-55   Examples and quotations from Robert Ordish, "Personal Impressions of a Machine Translation System," *The Incorporated Linguist,* Summer 1984.

p. 56   The translation comparison from the film *Chariots of Fire,* was found in an internal memorandum of Transtelex Limited.

pp. 57-58   Jack Smith, *The Pullet Surprise,* Franklin Watts, New York, 1982, p. 3.

p. 59   See reference in these notes at pp. 31-34 for information on the *Directory of Translators and Translation Services.*

p. 61   The "Creative Sightseeing" press release was received by one of the authors.

p. 66   The quote from *The Tulsa Tribune* was reproduced in *Linguistic Evidence,* by William M. O'Barr, 1982, Academic Press, p. 4.

p. 69   The information on the in-house French translator was derived from a proprietary source.

"A CHECKLIST FOR CHOOSING A PROFESSIONAL TRANSLATION SERVICE"

pp. 73-74   Comments on the differences among freelance translators, translation agencies, and full-service firms comes in part from *Language Monthly,* a British professional journal. *Language Monthly* refers to translation agencies as "envelope changers".

pp. 77-95   Most of the Checklist has been created from the day-to-day experience of Transtelex Limited in London and its U.S. representatives, Harris/Ragan Management Corporation of Los Angeles and Washington, D.C.

pp. 90-92   The comments on the comparative length of languages to express the same thought was taken from *Better Translation for Better Communication* and from *Computer Weekly,* mentioned above at pp. 31-34.

"SOME CONCLUDING THOUGHTS ABOUT COMMERCIAL TRANSLATIONS"

P. 104   The O'Barr quotations come from page 3 of his book referenced above at notes for p. 59.

p. 105   The quote from Boris Pasternak was found in an essay called "Translating Shakespeare". The essay appears in his 1959 book *I Remember,* translated by Manya Harari.

Although we did not use a lot of the material we found in other books and articles we reviewed, two concluding thoughts come to mind:

> • Roger Bacon is quoted in a book entitled *The Name of the Rose* by Umberto Eco as having said that "the conquest of learning is achieved through the knowledge of languages".

The fact that such a meaningful quotation comes to our attention by way of Eco's translator, William Weaver, suggests again the role of the translator in making the wisdom of people who write in one language available to those who understand another.

• We also think interested readers would appreciate Lord Woodhouselee's 18th century *Essay on the Principles of Translation*. He notes, for example, that "the genius of the Translator should be akin to that of the original author".

Although Lord Woodhouselee is clearly referring to literary translators, we think he might agree that the same sentiment now applies equally well to commercial translators.

COMMERCIAL TRANSLATIONS

INDEX

COMMERCIAL TRANSLATIONS

INDEX

M

Printed in Great Britain